Ten |
about

ex libris

Candlestick Press

Published by:
Candlestick Press,
Diversity House, 72 Nottingham Road, Arnold, Nottingham UK NG5 6LF
www.candlestickpress.co.uk

Design and typesetting by Diversity Creative Marketing Solutions Ltd.,
www.diversity.agency

Printed by Ratcliff & Roper Print Group, Nottinghamshire, UK

Selection and Introduction © John Greening, 2018

Cover illustration © David&Rews, 2018

Candlestick Press monogram © Barbara Shaw, 2008

© Candlestick Press, 2018

ISBN 978 1 907598 62 3

Acknowledgements:

The poems in this pamphlet are reprinted from the following books, all by
permission of the publishers listed unless stated otherwise. Every effort has
been made to trace the copyright holders of the poems published in this book.
The editor and publisher apologise if any material has been included without
permission or without the appropriate acknowledgement, and would be glad
to be told of anyone who has not been consulted. Thanks are due to all the
copyright holders cited below for their kind permission:

Fleur Adcock, *Poems 1960-2000* (Bloodaxe Books, 2000)

Alison Brackenbury, *Then* (Carcanet Press, 2013) by permission of the
publisher on behalf of the author

John Greening, 'The Better 'Ole' first published in this pamphlet, by
permission of the author

Stuart Henson, *London Grip* (Winter 2017/18) by kind permission of the
author

Kathleen Jamie, *The Bonniest Companie* (Picador, 2015)

Derek Mahon, *New Selected Poems* (Gallery Press, 2016) By kind permission
of the author and The Gallery Press, Loughcrew, Oldcastle, County Meath,
Ireland

John McAuliffe, *The Way In* (Gallery Press, 2015) By kind permission of the
author and The Gallery Press, Loughcrew, Oldcastle, County Meath, Ireland

MR Peacocke, *Caliban Dancing* (Shoestring Press, 2011)

Carol Rumens, *Poems 1968 - 2004* (Bloodaxe Books, 2004) by kind
permission of the author

Vernon Scannell, *Collected Poems 1950 - 1993* (Faber, 1998) by kind
permission of the Estate of Vernon Scannell

Where poets are no longer living, their dates are given.

All permissions cleared courtesy of Swift Permissions
(swiftpermissions@gmail.com)

Contents

Introduction

It's hard to resist peering into a shed. What might such a humble exterior conceal...?

Fans of TV crime drama will recognise the scenario. But poets have been gazing at cobwebby glass, trying locks, imagining dim interiors, since – well, probably since Tu Fu's 'pavilion by the river' back in the T'ang Dynasty. There's a particular allure for those of us not lucky enough to have a pavilion, lodge, summerhouse or grotto to write in. From Thoreau's Walden to Shaw's Corner to Dylan Thomas's Laugharne, sheds of one kind or another have provided a bolt-hole, perhaps even a bee-loud glade.

The *sh-* word used to be considered unpoetic. Huts were acceptable, and Yeats allowed himself a cabin at Innisfree, but Kipling was probably the first to praise 'tool- and potting-sheds'. Nowadays, poets visit B&Q like everybody else, unashamed to call a shed a shed – indeed, it's the title of more than one recent book of poetry.

Central to this anthology is Derek Mahon's masterly meditation on a dark secret life in rural Ireland. It's a poem to enter and sit inside, letting your senses gradually adjust – a little unnerving, but sheds can have that effect. Children are especially susceptible, as we see in Vernon Scannell's 'Hide and Seek' and in my own Nissen hut sonnet. More often, a shed offers a collection of curiosities, personal relics from a man-cave – like those handled here so lovingly by Alison Brackenbury, Stuart Henson and Carol Rumens. But Kathleen Jamie's is an 'arbour', a place of idyllic escape; Fleur Adcock's is preserved in the smell of creosote; MR Peacocke simply admires the paint on hers. And all the while, John McAuliffe hauls one up the garden path.

Enjoy whatever you find in the dusty half-light of *Ten Poems about Sheds*. But remember to leave the door ajar.

John Greening

Hide and Seek

Call out. Call loud: 'I'm ready! Come and find me!'
The sacks in the toolshed smell like the seaside.
They'll never find you in this salty dark,
But be careful that your feet aren't sticking out.
Wiser not to risk another shout.
The floor is cold. They'll probably be searching
The bushes near the swing. Whatever happens
You mustn't sneeze when they come prowling in.
And here they are, whispering at the door;
You've never heard them sound so hushed before.
Don't breathe. Don't move. Stay dumb. Hide in your blindness.
They're moving closer, someone stumbles, mutters;
Their words and laughter scuffle, and they're gone.
But don't come out just yet; they'll try the lane
And then the greenhouse and back here again.
They must be thinking that you're very clever,
Getting more puzzled as they search all over.
It seems a long time since they went away.
Your legs are stiff, the cold bites through your coat;
The dark damp smell of sand moves in your throat.
It's time to let them know that you're the winner.
Push off the sacks. Uncurl and stretch. That's better!
Out of the shed and call to them: 'I've won!
Here I am! Come and own up I've caught you!'
The darkening garden watches. Nothing stirs.
The bushes hold their breath; the sun is gone.
Yes, here you are. But where are they who sought you?

Vernon Scannell (1922 – 2007)

Shed
for Peter Fallon

I bought the shed, for a song, off a neighbour
who'd stopped using it after he paved the garden.
He'd inherited it or got it somewhere he couldn't remember,
not that I gave a second thought to its origin.

It was heavier than it looked so he helped take the roof to pieces.
After an hour prying out each crooked tack
we levered off its grey-green sandpaper stiffness
and rested it, on the drive, like a book stranded on its back.

The neighbour, looking at his watch, said, 'Let's push',
and the four walls and floor did move – a little.
In front of the garage, sweating, feeling each
ounce of the previous night, we saw too late

it was too big to go through. We counted the nails but couldn't:
they were like stars, more the more we looked. 'Heave it over,'
over the garage and down, he joked,
the garden path to its resting place under the magnolia.

No joke: we made a ramp of the ladder and inched
this half-tonne pine crate up and out of the road.
The scraped-flat garage roof pitched
under our careful feet. Two euphoric beers later, after we'd lowered

it into into place, we agreed on twenty quid. Every so often
he still calls in: today he's selling up and getting out.
He asks about the shed. I say it's fine, so half hidden
by April gusts of leaf and petal he can hardly see it,

as we look, out the window, at where it leans
against the fence, painted green, the unlocked door
opening on the lawnmower and half-full cans
of paint and petrol, pure potential, evaporating into the air.

But work makes work: paving the lot, he volunteers, makes more sense.
I'm offering him a cup of tea
when, before he can collect himself, he starts to resent
the twenty quid and leaving the shed behind: 'It was,' he says, 'almost free.'

John McAuliffe

The Shed

Step in it's a tardis: vortex of smells
distilled a century – of pre-war
timber, earth-floor, and the gold decay
of sawdust, linseed, two-stroke oil.

Is this what happens, then? All falls
in place as you're sucked down
through boards and beams, the sun's migraine
toward some backward ebb of space

by webs of rope-slack, amber panes
that seem to stain long afternoons
left there alone, lost to make sense
of time's great centrifuge, its huge mistake.

Now while you shrink to half your size
bemused by beetle-sift, hammocks of flies
you marvel at the fat bench vice
haunched like a Buddha on its height –

that and the square-tanked Velocette
you scramble on and don scuffed
gauntlets, goggles, Biggles-eyed,
throat-rev the throttle, ease the brake…

Behind, dry wallflowers and trellises,
tall shadows reaching to embrace…
Kick down my canny lad. Accelerate.
Back to the future and its great escape.

Stuart Henson

Creosote

What is it, what is it? Quick: that whiff,
that black smell – black that's really brown,
sharp that's really oily and yet rough,

a tang of splinters burning the tongue,
almost as drunkening as hot tar
or cowshit, a wonderful ringing pong.

It's fence-posts, timber yards, the woodshed;
it bundles you into the Baby Austin
and rushes you back to early childhood.

It's Uncle's farm; it's the outside dunny;
it's flies and heat; or it's boats and rope
and the salt-cracked slipway down from the jetty.

It's brushes oozing with sloshy stain;
it's a tin at the back of the shed: open it,
snort it! You can't: the lid's stuck on.

Fleur Adcock

To the Shipbuilder, his Tabernacle

Leave the shed-door open:
It's all that lights the garden once we've crossed
Your solstice-shaded birthday.
Dusty martyrs' crowns on the young ivy
Are the best we can do for autumn flowers:
Our rooftop-transept banishes the sunbeds
To Evensong by four.
But this door has a forest's eyes; when cedar
Bristles back to its origins, the day
Sticks like honey, never wants to let go.

Did we know we were buying sunlight,
Driving out to one of those desolate
Life-style hangars on the edge of town,
Strolling the wooden shtetl?
It was your birthday. I was feeling rich.
As if I'd been stockpiling English dreams
For the first Ukrainian-Jewish-Russian-Finn
Who'd crossed the border into B and Q.
I wrote a cheque to make the best and dearest
More yours than Moscow.

You got inside at once, opening crystals
Of space with a submariner's
Eye for horizons, deep in stacking-systems.
Tools lined the decks like sailors,
Some bright, some sleepy. Rusty captains stowed
Their wooden legs upright. Tins on tins,
Labelled *almond cake, pitted olives, ikra,*
Rattled with machine-food.
You pinched the nameplate from your office door
When they 'retired' you, fixed it to the shed.

And if the wood by now
Is being turned by micro-organisms,
Glued with a frost of cobwebs,
The gentle molecules of oil and creosote
Tired of stretching: if I submit and say
That autumn's pollen, halo-ing the ivy,
Was gold enough, more than we could have asked for,
Don't go before I've told you, with a wife's sad humour –
Leave the shed door open
So that I'll sometimes see you.

Carol Rumens

Paint

I like the way old paint
forgets itself, abandons
purpose: splits, peels,
curls, reveals what it was meant
to cover. Frost, wind, sun,
pick at its scales.

The shed door, for instance –
when it was new
what was it called? The Necessary?
Lavvy? Privy? – its warped stance
layered with stubborn blue,
indigo flaking to green, green to grey

to tattered ochre; deepest in
you glimpse the grained and naked board,
its staring cyclops knot.
Concealment, preservation
and each attempt at order
has warped to fantasy, a ragged art.

MR Peacocke

The Shed

He looked after tools, not just his own,
palm-polished handles, Victorian elm,
stamped with initials for John Maidens Barnes

my grandmother's father, who never bought farms,
but his own clutch of ditch-tools. Reach down the hoe

a blacksmith beat for the left-handed twist
of his father, the shepherd, who weeded bean rows
in after-work dazzle, the pipe's long blue mist.

How far they have travelled. This death is still raw.
Shallots' small worlds, held by knots of string,

spin as I brush them. I unhook the fork
he had wiped clean. Soil's finest grains cling.
Though I know it is sun, swept through glass, over land,

the handle grips hot as his palm to my hand.

Alison Brackenbury

A Disused Shed in Co. Wexford

Let them not forget us, the weak souls among the asphodels.
– Seferis, Mythistorema

(for JG Farrell)

Even now there are places where a thought might grow –
Peruvian mines, worked out and abandoned
To a slow clock of condensation,
An echo trapped for ever, and a flutter
Of wild flowers in the lift-shaft,
Indian compounds where the wind dances
And a door bangs with diminished confidence,
Lime crevices behind rippling rain-barrels,
Dog corners for bone burials;
And in a disused shed in Co. Wexford,

Deep in the grounds of a burnt-out hotel,
Among the bathtubs and the washbasins
A thousand mushrooms crowd to a keyhole.
This is the one star in their firmament
Or frames a star within a star.
What should they do there but desire?
So many days beyond the rhododendrons
With the world waltzing in its bowl of cloud,
They have learnt patience and silence
Listening to the rooks querulous in the high wood.

They have been waiting for us in a foetor
Of vegetable sweat since civil war days,
Since the gravel-crunching, interminable departure
Of the expropriated mycologist.
He never came back, and light since then
Is a keyhole rusting gently after rain.
Spiders have spun, flies dusted to mildew
And once a day, perhaps, they have heard something –
A trickle of masonry, a shout from the blue
Or a lorry changing gear at the end of the lane.

There have been deaths, the pale flesh flaking
Into the earth that nourished it;
And nightmares, born of these and the grim
Dominion of stale air and rank moisture.
Those nearest the door grow strong –
'Elbow room! Elbow room!'
The rest, dim in a twilight of crumbling
Utensils and broken pitchers, groaning
For their deliverance, have been so long
Expectant that there is left only the posture.

A half century, without visitors, in the dark –
Poor preparation for the cracking lock
And creak of hinges; magi, moonmen,
Powdery prisoners of the old regime,
Web-throated, stalked like triffids, racked by drought
And insomnia, only the ghost of a scream
At the flash-bulb firing-squad we wake them with
Shows there is life yet in their feverish forms.
Grown beyond nature now, soft food for worms,
They lift frail heads in gravity and good faith.

They are begging us, you see, in their wordless way,
To do something, to speak on their behalf
Or at least not to close the door again.
Lost people of Treblinka and Pompeii!
'Save us, save us,' they seem to say,
'Let the god not abandon us
Who have come so far in darkness and in pain.
We too had our lives to live.
You with your light meter and relaxed itinerary,
Let not our naive labours have been in vain!'

Derek Mahon

The Better 'Ole

An air-raid shelter from the Second War –
it was 'the shed' to me, the very soul
of Dad's dark silence.   Above the door
Grandpa had painted words (a kind of droll
remembrance) from the Bairnsfather cartoon,
those faces peering through a barrage, *Well,*
if you knows of a better 'ole... And soon
they'd gone, the two of them, a man-size shell
I should have spotted. Was it then my own
dark places blinded me? Lying awake
I'd hear what they kept down there start to drone
and turn to panto, climbing with a rake
in search of my voracious border, thud,
thud, fee fi fo, always smelling the blood.

John Greening

Arbour

A sea-side arbour, a garden shanty,
knocked together out of driftwood and furnished
with a beat-up sofa
                    is where I sit,
striving to cultivate the strandline's

take-it-or-leave-it attitude, and happy to remain
till the last young blackbird
                              flies the nest
lodged in the dog-rose to my left.

From time to time father bird
hops across our common square of grass,
                                cocking his head.
Friend, it's the sea you hear, vast and just
beyond those dunes, beyond your blackbird's ken,

but what do I know? May is again pegged out
across the whole northern hemisphere, and today
is my birthday. Sudden hailstorms sting
this provisional asylum. We are not done yet.

Kathleen Jamie